TREASU

WRITER'S JOURNAL

SEA OF WONDER

Acknowledgments appear on page 56.

Printed in the United States of America

ISBN 0-15-301273-0
12 13 030 03 02 01

HARCOURT BRACE & COMPANY
Orlando Atlanta Austin Boston San Francisco Chicago Dallas New York
Toronto London

CONTENTS

1 CREATURES

2 PUZZLERS

Writer's Handbook
57–66

UNIT ONE

CREATURES

Read about some "Creatures." Then turn to page 6.

GLUSCABI AND THE WIND EAGLE

"Grandmother," Gluscabi said, "What makes the wind blow?"

Grandmother Woodchuck looked up from her work.

"Gluscabi," she said, "Why do you want to know?"

Then Gluscabi answered her just as every child in the world does when they are asked such a question.

"Because," he said.

Grandmother Woodchuck looked at him. "Ah, Gluscabi," she said. "Whenever you ask such questions I feel there is going to be trouble. And perhaps I should not tell you. But I know that you are so stubborn you will never stop asking until I answer you. So I shall tell you. Far from here, on top of the tallest mountain, a great bird stands. This bird is named Wuchowsen, and when he flaps his wings he makes the wind blow."

from *Keepers of the Earth: Native American Stories and Environmental Activities for Children* by Michael J. Caduto and Joseph Bruchac

Snake!

What would happen if you found a snake in school?

We were thinking up words that rhyme with "lake," and I was just about to say "cake," when Kevin came running out of the bathroom yelling,

"Snake!"

"Kevin! I'm surprised at you!" said Mrs. Peloki. "You took Stephanie's turn. Raise your hand if you have something to say."

"But Mrs. Peloki," Kevin's voice was shaking. "I'm trying to tell you. *Snake.* There's a snake in the boys' bathroom."

You can watch the whole class panic—and track the snake down—in *Mrs. Peloki's Snake* by Joanne Oppenheim.

from *Mrs. Peloki's Snake* by Joanne Oppenheim

Something Big Has Been Here

Something big has been here,
what it was, I do not know,
for I did not see it coming,
and I did not see it go,
but I hope I never meet it,
if I do, I'm in a fix,
for it left behind its footprints,
and they are size fifty-six.

from *Something Big Has Been Here* by Jack Prelutsky

Write About Creatures

You can...

...write a story about the secret pet Pat Pinkle keeps in a cardboard box.

...report from the planet Fuzzwuzz. Describe the strange creature that lives there.

...tell about tracking a creature with footprints as big as a wading pool.

Ideas by ______________________________

(your name)

who?

Imagine that you are the owl in "Owl Moon." Who or what did you see and hear the night of the owling? What did you think?

The Owl ______________________
(your name)

CRASH!

Toot- Toot- Tweet

YEOWL!

BEHIND THE DOOR

What happened behind the door? Think about it. Then complete all the sentences.

First, I heard a yeowl behind the door.

That made me jump and then I hear a Crash.

CRASH!

Then, I went to my front door and heard a loud woof behid the door.

Next, I ran away from my door as fast I could run.

After that, I heard toot!- toot!- tweet! So I went back to my door.

I am sorry to say that next, I heard He-He-He-He and I Kew someone was laughing at me and I got mad and then I heard another crash.

WOOF

HE-HE-HE-HE

Finally, I opened my door and saw a boy with a bird and a dog and I said, "Sorry we're closed."

by Sarah Circe
(your name)

Teacher for a Day

Crinkleroot is going to be your teacher for a day. What would you like him to teach you? Fill out the lesson plan.

LESSON PLAN

Date ....   Teacher: Mr. Crinkleroot

Today we will study ....

....

....

....

Questions to answer ....

....

....

....

Activities ....

....

....

....

Students

....
(your name)

FIONNE MEOVOE

CEIFAN IEONOEVFOI

NFOIEICO PIOEDNFE

Doctor Do-a-Lot

Doctor Do-a-Lot is never bored! Doctor Do-a-Lot always has ideas about things to do. Imagine that you are Doctor Do-a-Lot, and help Julian, Huey, and Gloria. Write ten ways to have fun on a hot summer day.

1. ______
2. ______
3. ______
4. ______
5. ______
6. ______
7. ______
8. ______
9. ______
10. ______

General Instructions Take one idea each day to a family member for permission before beginning.

Making Friends with a Frog

Sandra and Jamal are best friends. Sandra says only facts. Jamal says only his opinions. Write what they say below.

written by ______________________________
(your name)

Finding Animal Facts

Think about what you read in "Animal Fact/Animal Fable." Observe an animal carefully. It may be a pet, a squirrel, an ant, or any other animal. Watch for at least 15 minutes. Write what you see, or your observations, below.

OBSERVER'S NOTEBOOK ______ (your name)

Animal Name ______

Description ______

Date ______ Where Seen ______

Time ______ Observations ______

______

______

One fact about this animal that my observations show is ______

______

Souvenir Shirt

Design a T-shirt that will help Armadillo remember one of the places he visited. After you have decorated your shirt, write about your designs.

Shirt designed by ______________________________

(your name)

About the Design:

____

____

____

If I Had WINGS

What would it be like to have wings? List your ideas on the notebook page below. Then use some of your ideas to write a poem about flying.

These are things I would see: ______

This is how I would feel: ______

A poem about flying: ______

by: ______ (your name)

A HOME FOR TOOKY

Kyo and his uncle George have different ideas about the best place for Tooky. Help them tell each other what they think. Be sure that they give reasons for their choices.

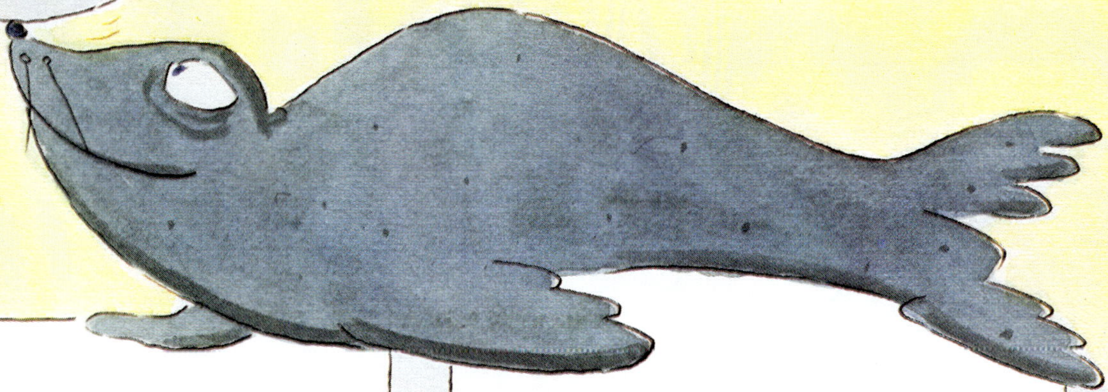

A zoo is a good place for a seal.

It is safe.

Tooky should live and swim freely

in the sea.

(your name)

Copilot

You are a modern pioneer. You are going deep into space to settle a new planet. You will be there for many years. But your rocket is very small. Only two people will fit. Luckily, you are able to choose your own copilot for the mission. Below is a picture of the person you chose. Write five words on the space suit that describe the person. Then have your copilot say a few sentences. Make the sentences show what the copilot is like.

by ______________________

(your name)

Seal World

If you could interview a seal, what questions would you ask about its world? Reread the poem "Seal" for ideas. Write your questions below.

Questions by ______________________________
(your name)

MAKING YOUR

IDEA PAD

1 STARTING UP A MAGAZINE

Sharpen your pencil. Gather your ideas. It's time to write, illustrate, and paste together a new magazine.

Remember, you are the Editor-in-Chief of this new magazine. You decide what this magazine is all about. To help you put your magazine together, look for the directions at the end of each unit in your book.

There are twelve colorful pages set aside for your magazine. Turn to page 69 to have a look. Be sure to read the Table of Contents on page 70. Notice how many different kinds of writing will be in your magazine. Glance at the rest of the pages. Imagine what you might write and draw on each one.

Do you know what your magazine will be about? Perhaps it will be about a special interest of yours. Perhaps your magazine will be a collection of a variety of ideas. Take some time to look through your favorite magazines. Brainstorm with a classmate. Write your ideas on your Idea Pad. When you have your magazine idea, complete this sentence:

My magazine will be about ____________________

OWN MAGAZINE

2 CHOOSING A NAME, CREATING A FRONT COVER

The name of a magazine is important. It should capture the idea of your magazine in just a few words. What will be the name of your magazine? Write down a list of possible names on another sheet of paper. Circle the one you like best.

The cover of a magazine is also important. How will your magazine cover catch the eye of your reader? How will your cover show what your magazine is all about? Try out your ideas on a sheet of paper before you make a final decision.

Sometimes magazine covers list some of the exciting articles in the magazine.

It is a way to say to readers, "Turn the page. Look inside."

Finished? Go to page 69 to publish your cover.

3 WRITING "A LETTER FROM THE EDITOR"

Often the editor of a magazine writes a letter to readers. The letter is a kind of invitation to sit back and enjoy reading the magazine. The letter also prepares readers for the stories and ideas they will soon read.

There is one page in your magazine set aside for the editor's letter. Since you are the editor, what will you write to your readers? How will you get your readers excited about the idea of your magazine? Write a draft of your letter. Ask a classmate to give you suggestions to make your letter even better.

Dear Readers,

You are sure to enjoy this magazine. Inside, you will find . . .

Finished? Go to page 71 to publish your letter.

MAKING YOUR

1 WRITING YOUR INFORMATION ARTICLE

Most magazines have articles that give their readers information. If a magazine is all about animals, then the article might be "How to Raise a Rabbit" or "Whose Paw Prints Are Those?" or "Is a Koala Bear a Bear?" What is your magazine all about? What information would you like to share with your readers? Choose a topic that you know a lot about. Be sure it's a topic you will enjoy writing about. Don't make a quick decision. Write down at least four ideas on your Idea Pad. Then circle the one you like best.

IDEA PAD

____

____

____

____

____

____

____

2 THINKING UP IDEAS

There are many ways to write an information article. Below are a few ideas that may help you think about your own article. Can you add another idea to the list? Write the idea that will work best for you.

- ✔ Make it funny.
- ✔ Write a serious report.
- ✔ Write a "how-to" guide.
- ✔ Create a photo report.
- ✔ Interview an expert.
- ✔ Interview yourself.

My idea is: ______________________________

____

____

Knowing *how* you will write your article will help you decide *what* information you need. If you are writing an interview, think about whom you will interview. If your article is funny, you will need to search for funny facts.

OWN MAGAZINE

Keep a "learning journal" as you collect facts. Write down facts that you may use in your article. Write why you think a fact is interesting. Write down other thoughts and feelings as you find information. All of these ideas will help you write your article.

3 GATHERING YOUR INFORMATION

What facts will you need before you can begin to write your article? Will you need to gather some new information? Take time to go to the library. Look for nonfiction books, magazines, newspapers, and encyclopedias for helpful information. Remember, classmates and family members have information too. Now look at all the information you have gathered. Which of these facts will most interest your readers? Write your article around these interesting facts.

4 DRAFTING AND REVISING; CHOOSING ILLUSTRATIONS

Are you ready to write a draft of your information article? Try out your ideas on a sheet of paper. Make your article as interesting to read as you can. When you are done with your draft, read it to a classmate. Ask for suggestions that will make your article even better.

There is plenty of space in your magazine to illustrate your article. Choose illustrations that will help your readers understand your article. You may want to include your own drawings, or cut out magazine and newspaper photos. You may also want to include captions below each illustration. One or two sentences will do.

Sometimes words are not enough. Pictures can often help readers understand an article better. Choose pictures that help explain important parts of your article. Charts and graphs are also helpful in showing information.

Ready to publish? Go to pages 72-73.

UNIT TWO

PUZZLERS

Read all about "Puzzlers."
Then turn to page 24.

Here's a puzzling riddle for you.

Judy said to the farmer, "We passed a man who was sleeping in a field under a tree. Who is he?" The farmer turned to Judy and said, "Brothers and sisters I have none, but that man's father is my father's son." Who is the man sleeping under the tree?

from *The Second Adler Book of Puzzles and Riddles* by Peggy Adler

The sleeping man is the farmer's son.

WISDOM

The emperor in China is sad. His little daughter is blind. He offers a reward to anyone who can help her to see. A wise old woodcarver says he has the answer.

Now when the guards arrived in the throne room of the Imperial Palace leading the old man by the arm, it happened that the emperor's blind daughter, Hwei Ming, was sitting by his side, her hands clasped before her, silent, sightless, and still. As the guards finished telling of the wonderful pictures carved on the golden stick, the princess clapped her hands.

"Oh, I wish I could see that wondrous stick," she said.

"Just so, just so," said the old man. "And I will show it to you. For it is no ordinary piece of wood, but a stick that sees."

from THE SEEING STICK by Jane Yolen
She's the same author who brought you the clever butler, Piggins.

Lives in winter,
Dies in summer
And grows with its root
upward!

(An icicle)

Traditional

Little Nanny Etticoat,
In a white petticoat,
And a red nose;
The longer she stands
The shorter she grows.

(A candle)

Traditional

Write About PUZZLERS

Write a puzzler.

You can...

...list 10 ways to move a heavy box from one room to another. Be creative!

...write a story about a clever pig who wants to get an apple from a high shelf.

...write three riddles and have someone else solve them.

by ____________________

(your name)

The African Traveler

Is a plain plain? Imagine that you are a travel writer. You write about faraway places. Right now, you are in a hot-air balloon, gliding over Ki-pat's home on the Kapiti Plain. Tell your readers what you see.

Where Am I?

Congratulations! You are an author! Meet two of your characters: Jake and Puffy. They are in a bit of trouble. They got lost in the desert. Your job is to write one or two paragraphs about what happened. There is just one catch: **You cannot mention that they are in the desert.** Write your paragraphs so readers can figure that out for themselves.

by ______________________________

(your name)

Penguin Poetry

These baby penguins live in a world of snow and ice. They are huddled against their parents' feet to stay warm. Think about the penguins and their world. What new pictures form in your mind? Write a poem. Make some of the lines rhyme.

by ______________________________

(your name)

Rainy Day Ideas

Reread the poem "Rainy Rainy Saturday."
Think of some things to do on a rainy day.
List them in the raindrops.

Now choose some of your ideas and write a poem about them.

THINGS TO DO ON A RAINY DAY

by ______________________
(your name)

FIRES OF THE FUTURE

Some people say that the next big fire in Yellowstone may not happen until after the year 2200. The world may be very different then. Imagine it is the year 2289, the time the next big fire is burning. You are a reporter flying over Yellowstone with your jet pack. Report on what happens.

This is ______________________________
(your name)

reporting live over Yellowstone Park.

Aunt Hettie is very generous. She is always buying things for you. The problem is, she only likes things that are purple! Write Aunt Hettie a letter. Try to convince her it would be better to buy the shoes on the right.

Dear Aunt Hettie,

Yours truly,

(your name)

The TV Library

This library will have a copy of every book that's been made into a video. The librarian needs a summary of each video. Write a summary of what happened in one of your favorite books. There's not much room! Your summary must tell the main events and still fit on the video box below.

summary by

____

(your name)

Safety First

The children in "Lon Po Po" got into trouble because they opened the door to a stranger. Mama left some rules to help them stay safe. Write some other safety rules they should follow.

Hi Kids!
Going to PoPo's house. I'll be home tomorrow. Please be sure to follow all our rules.
Love, Mama

Don't open the door to strangers

FAMILY NOTES

PLEASE DO	DON'T

rules by ______________________
(your name)

WHO ARE YOU?

Is this creature mean? Angry? Shy? Hungry? Is this girl scared? Brave? Silly? Helpful? Let's find out. Pretend they talk with each other. Write what they might say. Don't forget the quotation marks!

written by ____________________

(your name)

BUMPER STICKERS

by ______________________________
(your name)

"Cricket and Mountain Lion" teaches that "bigger doesn't mean better." Did it teach you anything about animals? About hard work? About solving problems? Write your ideas on a piece of scrap paper. Then make a bumper sticker. Write a clever saying about something the verse said to you.

Now write two more clever sayings for bumper stickers you think might be helpful for drivers to see.

THE BIG RACE

Imagine that Mountain Lion and Cricket held a race to settle their argument. You are going to announce the race for the big crowd that gathers to watch. Finish the speeches to tell about each racer.

LADIES and GENTLEMEN!

Welcome to the big race!
From California, wearing the gold shorts, the Mighty Mountain Lion!

Mr. Lion ______________________________

____

____

____

____

____

And wearing the red shorts ______________________________

____

____

____

____

____

____

____

Announcements by ______________________________
(your name)

Be a SECRET AGENT

Olivia Sharp likes to solve people's problems, but she also has a problem of her own. Be a secret agent. Decide what Olivia's problem is and how to solve it. Then write some notes for your file.

Agent for Secrets

Notes for the File on Olivia Sharp by________________________
(your name)

Olivia's secret problem is ________________________

How I solved it: ________________________

____

STEP 1 ________________________

____

STEP 2 ________________________

____

STEP 3 ________________________

____

Follow-up needed: ________________________

Message to myself: ________________________

Private Detective Wanted

Imagine that since you solved the missing chocolate chip cookie mystery, you have received too many cases to handle. Hire an assistant to help you solve mysteries. First, think about what kind of assistant you need. Take some notes on the form below. Then complete the Help Wanted Ad.

My Notes

Jobs to be done: ______________________

____

____

Kind of person needed to do those jobs:

____

____

____

Kind of person I enjoy working with:

____

____

____

HELP WANTED

Assistant Detective

To apply, please contact:

____

(your name)

MAKING YOUR

1 WRITING A STORY

Do you have an idea for a story? There are two magazine pages set aside for you to weave your idea into an imaginative tale. Ideas for stories often come from experiences we have had. We remember these experiences because they were important to us. We still remember how we felt—angry, joyful, or perhaps terribly scared. Think about experiences you have had that would make a good story. Look through your journal. Write down some of those ideas on your Idea Pad. Think about which idea has the power to be a good story.

IDEA PAD

2 Thinking About Story Ideas

Writing a story is like doing an experiment. In the beginning you are not quite sure what will happen. Try this writing experiment. Think about your story idea. Add a spark of imagination. Then turn that story idea into a—fairy tale. What does your story idea look like now? Try another experiment. Turn your story idea into a—mystery. Now what does your story look like? Experimenting with different story forms is a creative way to discover story ideas.

On a separate sheet of paper, draw three boxes. For each box, choose a story form. Experiment with your story idea using each story form you chose. Decide which of your ideas will make the best story for your magazine.

STORY FORM: ANIMAL
STORY IDEA: TWO SQUIRRELS MEET IN A TREE.

STORY FORM: FUNNY
STORY IDEA: TWO ALIENS MEET ON MARS

STORY FORM: MYSTERY
STORY IDEA: STRANGERS IN A HOUSE

OWN MAGAZINE

3 PLANNING YOUR STORY

Take an imaginary walk through your story. What happens at each step?

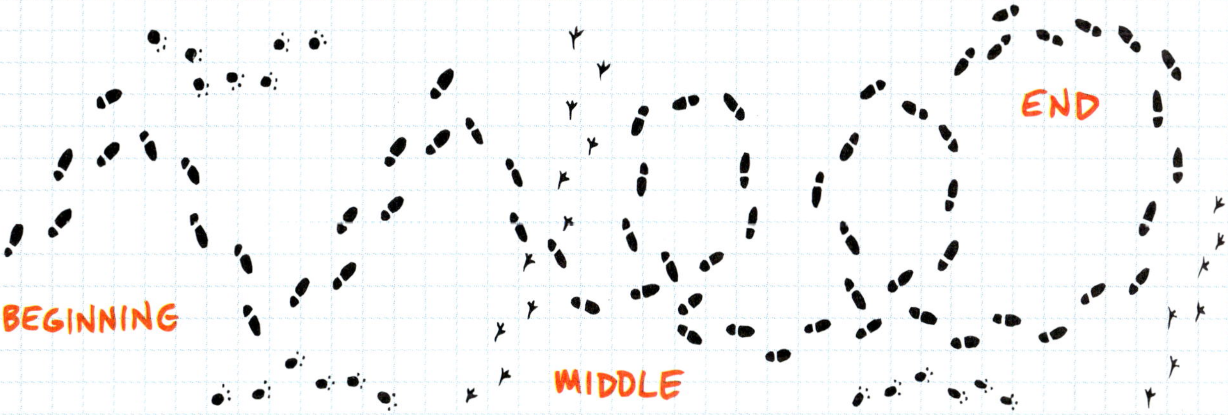

4 DRAFTING AND REVISING YOUR STORY

Are you ready to try out all of your ideas for your story? On a separate sheet of paper, write a draft. Experiment with your words. How will you describe your characters so that your readers see them clearly? How will you write your story so that your readers are eager to find out what happens? When you have finished, read your draft to a classmate. Does your classmate have suggestions that will make your story even better?

Would you like to illustrate your story? There is plenty of room for pictures on your magazine pages. You may want to draw your own pictures, or cut out magazine and newspaper photos. Turn to pages 74 and 75 to plan these magazine pages.

Good stories have good characters. As a reader, you really care about what happens to those characters. You can picture just how they look. You can "hear" how they talk. You know how they are feeling. Think about how you can make your readers *care* about your characters.

Ready for the next steps? Go to pages 74-75 to publish your story.

UNIT THREE MEMORIES

Read all about "Memories."
Then turn to page 42.

Memories of Grandpa

Grandpa had some goldfish. He kept them in the big water trough. Every day he fed them oatmeal. Sometimes he let me scatter the oatmeal on the water. Just enough! Not too much! With all that food to eat and all that room to swim, the fish grew longer than a grown-up's hand.

Do you suppose the cows were surprised when they put their heads down to drink water and looked right straight in the face of a huge goldfish?

You can read about more memories in *Grandpa Had a Windmill, Grandma Had a Churn* by Louise A. Jackson.

Finding Lost Memories

Wilfrid Gordon has lots of friends at the old people's home next door. His special friend is Miss Nancy.

One day Wilfrid Gordon heard his mother and father talking about Miss Nancy.

"Poor old thing," said his mother.

"Why is she a poor old thing?" asked Wilfrid Gordon.

"Because she's lost her memory," said his father.

"It isn't surprising," said his mother. "After all, she is ninety-six."

Wilfrid Gordon makes up his mind to help Miss Nancy find her memories in *Wilfrid Gordon McDonald Partridge* by Mem Fox.

Birthdays!

Rosa has a party in her back yard on her birthday every year. Her father hangs a ***piñata*** in the tree, and her friends and family try to break it. The children can't wait to hit the large papier-mâché figure, which is covered with bright tissue paper and filled with candies. They take turns hitting it with a broomstick until it breaks. When the candies tumble out, the children scramble for them. Then everyone eats ***tacos***, ***tamales***, and ***frijoles***, or pinto beans, and other foods. Of course, there's always a birthday cake.

from *Texans: A Story of Texan Cultures for Young People* by Barbara Evans Stanush

WRITE ABOUT

MEMORIES

You can...

...imagine a memory. Be a bird. Write about hatching and learning to fly.

...write a memory of your childhood for your grandchildren to read.

...write a poem. Be yourself or an older person. Begin each line: I remember...

by ____________________
(your name)

The Family Museum NEWSLETTER

You are a writer for The Family Museum's newsletter. "The Patchwork Quilt" is the newest museum exhibit. Write an article that describes the quilt, tells who loaned it to the museum, and gives other information about it.

article written by ______________________________
(your name)

Hello

Your big brother Bud is calling about his camping trip. Everyone in the family wants to hear, but there is only one phone. Listen to Bud. Then tell the family what he says, in a shorter form. Keep it quick! It's a long distance call!

Bud says: Hi, Sprout! You wouldn't believe this phone! It's about a zillion years old, and it's nailed to a pine tree in the middle of the woods!

You say: ____

____

Bud says: My tent got knocked down last night. Guess what did it? Well, it is hairy, likes honey, and weighs about 800 pounds! It scared itself when the tent fell, and it ran away.

You say: ____

____

Bud says: Boy, do I love hiking all day and setting up camp at night! I never had so much fun, and I met this other guy who likes model trains as much as I do!

You say: ____

____

Bud says: Good-bye ____________________________
(your name)

You say: ____

Passing It On

The people in the poem "Tradition" learned how to balance things from their families and friends, not from books. Everyone learns some things that way. How did you learn the rules to your games or the words to jump-rope verses? What else have you learned that was passed on to you by others? Make a list of those things.

My name:

Things people passed on to me:

1.

2.

3.

4.

5.

6.

7.

It's Showtime

Grandpa, the Song and Dance Man, will give a show at your school to raise money for school clubs. Make a poster to advertise the show.

Poster by ______________________________
(your name)

The Dancer

Look at the picture of the dancer. Then complete each sentence.

Dancer, your feet whirl like ____________________
____
____.

Dancer, your legs are strong and sure as __________
____
____.

Your arms are branches and your hands are ____________________
____
____.

You are a ______________________________ leaping through the air.

Dancer, your dress floats like a ____________________
____
____.

Dancer, your dance is as beautiful as a ____________________
____.

by ______________________________
(your name)

Time Capsule

The poet in "Drums of My Father" feels at one with all time, both the past and the future. Help the poet leave a message for her children's children, and for all future people. Fill the time capsule with things that show what our present-day world is like.

My Time Capsule

____
(your name)

CONTENTS	A message to our children's children

Hello from the 1990s

YOU FOUND IT!

Mel Fisher searched for 20 years before he found his treasure. Do you think it was worth it? Imagine that you searched with Mr. Fisher for those 20 years. Answer the interview questions below.

Audience, we have with us

______________________________, who
(your name)

searched for 20 long years for sunken treasure.

What was your life like for those 20 years? Didn't you have to give up a lot to search for treasure?

What will you do now? How will your life be different?

Do you think it was worth it?

Display Your Dinosaur

A Picture of ______________________
(dinosaur's name)

Imagine you have discovered a kind of dinosaur. What does it look like? What does it eat? How does it walk? Make up a name for your dinosaur. Draw a picture of it, and then write about it.

About this dinosaur: ______________________

____

____

____

____

____

____

____

Designed by: ______________________
(your name)

FIND FUN ON LOST ISLAND

Imagine that you are a travel agent. Develop a tourist guide to the lost island found by the boy who sailed the *Zephyr*. Describe the island so travelers will want to visit it.

Come to Lost Island!

Lose your troubles!

by ____________________
(your name)

Reading for the Senses

Answer the questions by writing a sentence to describe each thing. Draw a picture with your words. (One is done for you.)

by ______________________________
(your name)

What do you see? Melted orange rock shot into the air like an upside-down waterfall.

What do you hear? The roar and hiss of the flames filled my ears.

What do you see? ______________________________

What do you smell? ______________________________

What do you hear? ______________________________

What do you feel? ______________________________

What do you see? ______________________________

What do you taste? ______________________________

The Ostrich needs a new way to fly because the other birds can't be around all the time to help. Draw an invention the Ostrich can use for flying. Then write directions for using it.

Presenting...From the Inventor's Club

Name of invention ____________________

Invented by ____________________
(your name)

How to use it:

MAKING YOUR

WRITING A RECIPE

Your readers have asked you to include your favorite recipe in your magazine. You may want to share a favorite family recipe or make up a new one. Maybe the subject of your magazine will give you an idea for a recipe.

Look through some cookbooks. Notice that recipes have two parts. The first part lists the ingredients and tells how much of each ingredient to use. Notice the abbreviations for measurements, such as *tsp* for *teaspoon* and *tbsp* for *tablespoon*.

Try out some of your ideas on a separate sheet of paper. Have fun illustrating your recipe with a big, beautiful picture.

Ready to publish? Go to pages 76–77.

WRITING AN ADVERTISEMENT

A company has asked if it can advertise a new product in your magazine. You think your readers would be interested in this new product. You agree as long as the advertisement is eye-catching and has clear information.

What is the product? Why would your readers be particularly interested in it? What does the ad look like? What catches your eye? Is it the big, bold lettering? Is it the pictures? Is it the clever name of the product? There is one page in your magazine for this advertisement. Sketch out some ideas on paper before you make a final decision.

Ready for the next steps? Go to page 78.

OWN MAGAZINE

COLLECTING RIDDLES AND JOKES

Which jokes and riddles will you include? First, make a list of all the riddles and jokes you think are funny. Read some good joke books. Ask your friends and family to tell you their favorite jokes.

List the ones you like best. When you are ready, circle the jokes and riddles you will "publish" in your magazine. Then decide which ones you will illustrate. Have fun putting this page together.

Ready to publish? Go to page 79.

FINISHING UP YOUR MAGAZINE

You are almost finished with your magazine. There are just three more things to do.

Complete Your Magazine's Table of Contents

Look at the Table of Contents page in your magazine. Write the name of each writing project on the correct line.

Design the Back Cover of Your Magazine

There is space on page 80 for your own design. You may want to draw a picture, or cut out magazine pictures to make a collage.

Take One Last Look Through Your Magazine

Add any finishing touches to your pages.

Go to page 70 to find the Table of Contents.

ACKNOWLEDGMENTS

Text Selections

For permission to reprint copyrighted material, grateful acknowledgment is made to the following sources:
Fulcrum Publishing, Inc., 350 Indiana St. #350, Golden, CO 80401: From p. 67 in *Keepers of the Earth: Native American Stories and Environmental Activities for Children* by Michael J. Caduto and Joseph Bruchac.
Greenwillow Books, a division of William Morrow & Company, Inc.: "Something Big Has Been Here" from *Something Big Has Been Here* by Jack Prelutsky. Text copyright © 1990 by Jack Prelutsky.

Photograph Credits

Tony Stone Worldwide 27; Harcourt Brace & Company Photo/Debi Harbin 31,36; Harcourt Brace & Company Photo/Britt Runion 37; The Bettmann Archive 40; Brent Jones 45; Harcourt Brace & Company Photo/Maria Paraskevas 46, top; Harcourt Brace & Company Photo/Britt Runion 46, bottom; MGM 47; George F. Lee/Woodfin Camp 52, top; Jack Daly 52, second left; Tony Arruza/Bruce Coleman 52, third left; H. Armstrong Roberts 52, bottom; Harcourt Brace & Company Photo 68

WRITER'S HANDBOOK

Robert Dale, Bernard Adnet, Stacey May, Janice Edelman 57-66

YOUR OWN MAGAZINE

Scott Matthews, Janice Edelman 67-80

WRITER'S HANDBOOK

This is the beginning of your Writer's Handbook. It has reminders about making your sentences, paragraphs, stories, and letters clear and correct.

The Handbook also has examples that show how other writers have used the reminders. As you work on your Magazine, check your Writer's Handbook. It will help you in the drafting, revising, and proofreading stages of the writing process.

WRITING SENTENCES

Capital Letters and End Punctuation

Every sentence begins with a capital letter and ends with an end mark.

Use a **period** at the end of a sentence that tells something.

Grandpa was a song and dance man who once danced on the vaudeville stage.

Use a **period** at the end of a sentence that gives an order or direction.

Follow them and see what they tell you.

Use a **question mark** at the end of a sentence that asks something.

Can you see an owl in this tree?

Use an **exclamation point** at the end of a sentence that shows strong feeling.

Finally, in 1970, he finds a clue!

Begin all important proper nouns with a capital letter.

Other Capital Letters

Names

Huey and Gloria grabbed their socks.

The names of **people and pets** are proper nouns.

In April and May of 1988, much more than the normal amount of rain fell.

The names of **days of the week, months of the year,** and **holidays** are proper nouns.

People came from such faraway places as Oslo, Innsbruck, and Banff to see Buford.

The names of **towns, cities, states,** and **countries** are proper nouns.

Mrs. Fridgeflake is home all the time.

Begin the **title of a person,** such as Miss or Dr., with a capital letter. The titles Mr., Ms., Mrs., and Dr. are abbreviations. Use a period after each of these titles.

Use a capital letter for an **initial** that takes the place of a name. Use a period after an initial.

Jackie was born in 1962 and named after President John F. Kennedy's wife, Jacqueline.

Once, while traveling along the seashore, I stopped at a small fishing village.

Write the **word I** as a capital letter.

COMMAS

A farm dog answered the train**, and** then a second dog joined in.

Use a comma **before** the word **and** when it joins sentences **in a compound sentence.**

Use commas **to separate words in a series.**

Look for signs animals leave in parks and woodlots**,** on pavements and sidewalks**,** under trees**,** around streams and ponds**,** and in the snow.

Well, I can't be right about everything.

Use a comma **after** the word ***yes, no,*** *or* ***well*** *at the beginning of a sentence.*

Direct Quotations

A direct quotation shows the exact words a speaker used.

Use **quotation marks** before and after a direct quotation.

"I've got to get rid of these things," she muttered.

Begin the **first word** in a direct quotation with a **capital letter.**

Then a voice said, "The world is coming to an end."

"The pizza was just an excuse," Desiree said.

Use a **comma between the words that tell who is speaking and a direct quotation.**

Use an **end mark before** the **closing quotation marks** of a direct quotation.

Use a **period** if the direct quotation tells something or gives an order or direction.

As George climbed on the snowmobile, Kyo said to his father, "I want to move her with the dog team."

Shang, who was the oldest, said through the latched door, "Who is it?"

Use a **question mark** if the direct quotation asks something.

Use an **exclamation point** if the direct quotation shows strong feeling.

We sit on one of Grandma's woolen blankets, clap our hands, and call out, "Yay, Grandpa!"

TITLES

Begin the first word, the last word, and each important word in a title with a capital letter.

Use quotation marks before and after the title of a story, a poem, or a song. Underline the title of a book.

The story about Kyo and Tooky comes from the book **The Secret of the Seal**.

APOSTROPHES

My brothers all said sometimes **there's** an owl and sometimes there **isn't**.

Use an apostrophe in place of the letter or letters that have been left out **in a contraction.**

Cradling the **seal's** head in his lap, he sang a song his mother used to sing to him.

Add an apostrophe and s to most **singular nouns** to show **possession.**

When the parade was over, the leader of the **teachers'** panel stood up.

Add an apostrophe to **plural nouns that end in s** to show **possession.**

SUBJECT-VERB AGREEMENT

Be sure that the present-time verb in a sentence agrees with the subject of the sentence. **If the subject is singular, add s or es to the verb.**

plural: Many more **years go** by.

singular: The **salvage goes** on for weeks, months, years.

WRITING PARAGRAPHS

Indent the first line of a paragraph.

Write **one sentence that tells the main idea of the paragraph.** This sentence is the **topic sentence** of the paragraph. Usually the topic sentence comes at the beginning of the paragraph.

> **Raccoons eat everything they can catch or find.** They even raid garbage cans. They come to the water to hunt for crayfish, frogs, snails, and freshwater clams.

Be sure all the other sentences in the paragraph add **details** about the main idea.

> Signs of renewal were already clear in the spring of 1989. Twenty kinds of grasses sprouted on the burned forest floor, mixed with flowers such as delicate shooting stars. The burned meadows grew more vigorously than before, with a healthy, deep green glow, nourished by nitrogen and other nutrients released by the fires. The new growth is not only healthy and green, it actually contains more nutrients for the animals like elk that eat it. Grazers prefer the grass and other plants in recently burned areas, and it makes them healthier than grass in unburned meadows.

WRITING LETTERS

BEGIN A LETTER with a heading.

- The heading should tell your address and the date.
- Begin street, city, and state names with capital letters.
- Use a comma between the names of your city and state.
- Also begin the name of the month with a capital letter.
- Use a comma after the number of the day.

USE A GREETING after the heading in a letter.

- Begin the word Dear with a capital letter.
- Begin the name of the person to whom you are writing with a capital letter.
- Use a comma at the end of the greeting.

END A LETTER with a closing and your signature.

- Begin the first word in the closing with a capital letter.
- Use a comma at the end of the closing.

7337 Wilmont Avenue
Flint, Michigan 48502
August 14, 1999

Dear Mr. and Mrs. Goldberg,

Thank you for taking me along on your family camping trip. I had a great time. I had never hiked so far before—or seen so many stars! It was terrific.

Your friend,
Clem

WRITING STORIES

Be sure your story has a **beginning**, a **middle**, and an **ending**.

In the **beginning**, tell about the story setting and characters. Give the characters a problem to solve.

In the **middle**, tell how the characters try to solve the problem.

In the **ending**, tell how the problem is finally solved.

Tell about the story events in the order in which they happened.

USING EDITING AND PROOFREADING MARKS

You can use these editor's marks when you revise and proofread your own writing.

- ≡ Use a capital letter.
- ⊙ Add a period.
- ∧ Add something.
- ∧, Add a comma.
- Add quotation marks.
- Cut something.
- Replace something.
- Transpose.
- Spell correctly.
- ¶ Indent paragraph.
- / Make a lowercase letter.

Geri ~~came~~ [rushed] into the house. ~~She was rushing.~~ ~~She~~ [and] gasped, "get me a ~~another~~ jar—quick!"

¶ Her father grabbed a clear jar ~~made out of~~ glass from a shelf handed it to her and asked, "What is it this time? Another spider?"

Geri grinned at her dad. ~~Then Geri~~ [as she] took the jar and raced out the door agian [again]. She called out and said, "no, this is even beter [better] than a spider. Just wait 'til [you] see it!" ~~There was excitement in her voice.~~

CHECK IT OUT

Make Your Own MAGAZINE

Now you have your magazine title...

PUBLISH!

Share it!

Show your list of magazine titles to a classmate. Decide together which title is best for your magazine.

Picture it!

Make a picture or find pictures or photos in old magazines or newspapers for your front cover.

Do it!

- Cut paper to cover the blue grid on this page.
- Put your pictures on the sheet of paper. Add your title in big, bold letters.
- Now attach the paper to the blue grid.

Before beginning, see pages 18–19.

contents

Before beginning, see page 55.

Now you have a draft of your introduction...

PUBLISH!

Write it!

Use your classmate's suggestions to revise your letter. Remember to introduce yourself.

Picture it!

Find a photograph of yourself or make a self-portrait.

Do it!

- Cut paper to cover the blue grid on this page.
- Write your letter on the sheet of paper. Add your photo or portrait. Sign your letter.
- Now proofread your letter and attach it to the blue grid.

"Letter from the editor" 3

Before beginning, see page 19.

Now you have a draft of your information article...

PUBLISH!

Name it!

Think of an interesting title. Make it funny or serious, depending on your subject.

Design it!

You have two pages for your information article. Plan how you want to use them. Decide where to put your pictures or illustrations. Write captions for them.

Do it!

- Cut papers to cover the blue grids on this page and the next one.
- Write your information article on the sheets of paper. Add your pictures and title.
- Now proofread your information article and attach it to the blue grids.

Before beginning, see pages 20–21.

information article

continues!

5

story

6

Now you have a draft of your story...

PUBLISH!

Name it!

Think of an interesting title for your story.

Design it!

You have two pages for your story. Plan how you want to use them. Decide where to put your pictures. Arrange them so they make your story come alive!

Do it!

- Cut papers to cover the blue grid on this page and the next one.
- Write your story on the sheets of paper. Add your pictures and your title.
- Now proofread your story and attach it to the blue grids.

Before beginning, see pages 38–39.

story

continues!

7

recipe

8

Now you have directions for your recipe...

PUBLISH!

Picture it!

Make pictures or find pictures or photos in old magazines or newspapers to illustrate your recipe. Illustrate ingredients, too.

Design it!

You have two pages for your recipe. Plan how you want to use them. Decide how to arrange your recipe directions with your illustrations. Make sure the directions are in order.

Do it!

- Cut papers to cover the blue grid on this page and the next one.
- Write your recipe on the sheets of paper. Add pictures or photos.
- Now proofread your recipe and attach it to the blue grids.

Before beginning, see page 54.

recipe

continues!

9

advertisement

10

Now you have a product to advertise...

PUBLISH!

Picture it!

How are you going to present your product to your readers? Decide whether to draw it, or to find pictures or photos in old magazines.

Plan it!

Sketch a plan for your advertisement. Will you use more than one picture? Will you use fancy letters for the name? Now add some sentences to "sell" the product.

Do it!

- Cut paper to cover the blue grid on this page.
- Put your pictures on the sheet of paper. Add your sentences and finishing touches.
- Now proofread your advertisement and attach it to the blue grid.

Before beginning, see page 54.

riddles and jokes

11

Now you have a draft of your riddles and jokes...

PUBLISH!

Name it!

Think of a funny name for your riddles and jokes page.

Draw it!

Create pictures for the jokes and riddles you chose to illustrate.

Do it!

- Cut paper to cover the blue grid on this page.
- Put your riddles and jokes on the sheet of paper. Add pictures and your title.
- Now proofread your riddles and jokes page and attach it to the blue grid.

Before beginning, see page 55.

back cover

Now you have ideas for your back cover...

PUBLISH!

Design it!

Decide how to use your drawings or pictures to make an eye-catching back cover.

Do it!

- Cut paper to cover the blue grid on this page.
- Put your pictures on the sheet of paper.
- Now attach your back cover to the blue grid.

Before beginning, see page 55.